DISCOVERING
GOD
IN YOU

A YOUNG WOMAN'S GUIDE *to* IDENTITY,
WORTH, PURPOSE, *and* FREEDOM

DISCOVERING GOD IN YOU

A YOUNG WOMAN'S GUIDE *to* IDENTITY, WORTH, PURPOSE, *and* FREEDOM

by:

KIMBERLEY J. RODNEY

Copyright © 2022 by Kimberley J. Rodney

All rights reserved. Except permitted under the U.S. Copyright Act of 1976, no part of this publication may be used, reproduced, distributed or transmitted by in any form or by any means, graphic, electronic or mechanical or stored in a database or retrieval system, without the prior written permission to the publisher except in the case of brief quotations embodied in critical articles and reviews.

This book is designed to provide information and motivation to our readers. It is sold with the understanding that the publisher is not engaged to render any type of medical, psychological, legal, or any other kind of professional advice. The content of each article is the sole expression and opinion of its author, and not necessarily that of the publisher. No warranties or guarantees "are expressed or implied by the publisher's choice to include any of the content in this volume. Neither the publisher nor the individual author(s) shall be liable for any physical, psychological, emotional, financial, or commercial damages, including, but not limited to, special, incidental, consequential or other damages. Our views and rights are the same: You are responsible for your own choices, actions, and results."

Unless otherwise indicated, Scriptures are taken from the Holy Bible, New International Version®, NIV® Copyright © 1973, 1978, 1984, 2011 by Biblica, Inc.™ Used by permission. All rights reserved worldwide.

Scripture quotations marked MSG are from The Message. Copyright © Eugene H. Peterson 1993, 1994, 1995, 1996, 2000, 2001, 2002 by Tyndale House Foundation. Used by permission of Tyndale House Publishers, Inc., Carol Stream, Illinois 60188. All rights reserved.

Scriptures quotations marked NKJV are from the New King James Version. Copyright © 1979, 1980, 1982, Thomas Nelson, Inc., Publishers. All rights reserved. Used by permission.

Scripture quotations marked NRSV are from the Revised Standard Version of the Bible, copyright © 1946, 1952, and 1971 National Council of the Churches of Christ in the United States of America. Used by permission. All rights reserved worldwide.

Vine Publishing's name and logo are trademarks of Vine Publishing, Inc.

ISBN: 978-1-7367483-6-7 (paperback)
ISBN: 979-8-9867471-2-5 (e-book)

Library of Congress Cataloging-in-Publication Data
Library of Congress Control Number: 2022915990

Published by Vine Publishing, Inc.
New York, NY
www.vinepublish.com

Printed in the United States of America

DEDICATION

I dedicate this book to my son Isaiah, my gift from God.

ACKNOWLEDGMENT

God, You have been my Rock and my Strength. Thank you for giving me purpose and adopting me into your Kingdom. I'm grateful to be called your daughter, Kimberley Juanita Rodney.

To my dear son, this book is your legacy—one that you will share with your family one day. It is a legacy that will help them know that putting God first will tremendously impact their lives.

To my family, thank you for always supporting me. Finally, I acknowledge my deceased father, Halibold Rodney. Although you are not here on this earth, I know for a fact that your spirit lives within me, and you are proud of the woman I have become.

TABLE OF CONTENTS

INTRODUCTION..xi

CHAPTER 1
  Loss: How The Journey Began 1

CHAPTER 2
  Discovering A New You 11

CHAPTER 3
  Discovering Your Worth 21

CHAPTER 4
  Discovering Your Purpose 31

CHAPTER 5
  Discovering Freedom 41

CHAPTER 6
  Soar! 51

INTRODUCTION

For most of my early adult life depression, insecurities, self-doubt and low self-esteem kept me from being who I was created to be. As a child, I was never told that I was smart, or beautiful, or if I just put my mind to it, I could be anything I wanted to be. I was never affirmed—never told that I was gifted or talented. I, as far as I believed, had nothing to offer society. To make things worse my father died when I was five, his loss was significant for many reasons, and it left a gaping hole that in my early twenties, I attempted to fill with attention from men.

The void that my father left was so massive that I did everything to try to fill it. I made bad choices, did reckless things, chose paths that weren't right for me, but nothing—or no one, seemed able to fill it...at least that's what I thought. I needed a father. I was missing a father, but I later realized that my Heavenly Father has always been there.

It took years for me to make the decision to draw closer to God, and in doing so, I realized that God was with me all along. While my earthly father is gone, God has protected me, covered me and taken care of me. God became my Father. God became my identity. I began to see myself the way He sees me. The journey has not been easy, but I can now say that I am beautiful, gifted and created with purpose.

Perhaps you have struggled with low self-esteem, depression and/or you don't believe that any good thing can come from your life. If you can relate, then I wrote this book for you. Discovering God in You was written for every young woman who has struggled with feeling as if they weren't enough.

I wrote this for the young girl who does not quite know who she is becoming. I wrote it for the young lady struggling with her identity. I wrote to remind you that you are not alone. I see you.

In this book, I will lead you through my journey from lost and broken to finding a new life and new future in my relationship with God. You will not only be given the tools to be the woman that God has called you to be, but I have also included scriptures. Throughout the book, I share many scriptures that I hold dear to my heart. One in particular that comes to mind, and one that I have written on my bathroom mirror is Jeremiah 29:11: "For I know the plans I have for you, declares the Lord, plans to prosper you and not to harm you, plans to give you hope and a future" (NIV). This scripture keeps me anchored to hope. In addition to the scriptures, I have provided positive affirmations. I believe that we all need words of encouragement, but especially during those early young adult years—those years of self-discovery.

As you read Discovering God in You, it is my prayer that

you will take the time to reflect on the content of each chapter. Meditate on the scriptures provided. Hold on to God's Word—take the time to meditate on it. Ask yourself, "What assurance is God giving me in this?" Spend time with God and in God's Word. Declare the affirmations provided over your life, and make sure to also write your own personal declarations in the space provided after each chapter. These affirmations have been impactful in my life, and today, at the age of 42, I can confidently declare, "Kimberley J. Rodney, you are ENOUGH." Now, let me say that I have not fully arrived. I am still on the journey towards unreserved self-love and acceptance. I have not arrived, but I am definitely not who I used to be.

My hope is that you see yourself throughout this book. I pray that it not only captures your mind, but your heart and soul. I hope that at the end of this book, you will discover that your identity is not found in material things or relationships—your identity is only found in God. The insights in this book, God's Word, and the affirmations provided were written in hopes that you will not make the same mistakes I did, but that you will flourish mentally and spiritually. I pray that when you get to the last chapter, you will know that you, young lady, are fearfully and wonderfully made (Psalm 139:14). You are God's masterpiece!

CHAPTER 1
LOSS: HOW THE JOURNEY BEGAN

He was a tall, lean, strong, kind-hearted man. I remember when I got my first bike and he took me out to Lincoln Park in Brooklyn, NY just so that I could practice. He was my dad and I was his little princess, Kimmy.

When my mom and I first migrated to New York from the island of Dominica, West Indies in 1983, I was only four years of age. When we arrived, we lived with my grandmother and my dad would always visit us. Eventually we would all move in together, as one family, in an apartment on Utica Avenue in Brooklyn. Life was good, but then things changed. Daddy wasn't himself anymore. He seemed weak—no energy, and would always wear a brown robe around the house. Something was different with my dad, and when I looked into his eyes all I saw as sadness. What my four-year-old mind did not realize at the time was that my daddy was sick.

I remember going to St. Mary's Hospital in Brooklyn with

my mom, and back then children weren't allowed in the room, even if the patient was your parent. So, my mom left me in the waiting room, and there I sat alone. We traveled in silence on the way home from the hospital. Ecclesiastes 3 reminds us that there is a time under the sun for everything, and in 1984 my dad's time to die had arrived. I was only five years of age.

I vividly remember the funeral. Dad was dressed in a blue suit, and there I was at the graveside chewing gum, somewhat detached from the significance of the event. My mom was heartbroken, and she sobbed uncontrollably as the casket went down into the earth. Her pain was real, and why wouldn't it be? There she was, a young mom in her twenties, now left only with the memories of the man she loved deeply—the man she believed would eventually be her husband, and the father of their growing family. Life had changed.

I can't remember ever having a significant conversation with my mom about what was happening. I can't remember my tears or sadness. Maybe I just didn't quite know what death was. I wasn't provided a safe space to discuss my dad's death, or maybe the adults in my life just didn't understand the importance of helping a child process loss. Regardless of the reason, what I do remember is that after my dad died, the feeling of loneliness dominated my life.

As a single working woman, my mom would leave me

home alone a lot after school. I was so young, and being left alone unsupervised was scary. I was a little girl riddled with anxiety and fear. There was no one with me—no friend, no companionship. I was alone and lonely. At age five, my dad's passing had triggered a barrage of losses—loss of a parent, loss of emotional connections with the adults around me, and an overall loss of a sense of security.

I experienced tremendous loss, but as I got older, I became lost. Dad's passing impacted my life tremendously throughout my teenage and young adult years. As a teenager trying to find myself, I defied my mom and stepfather's rules about not having a boyfriend. I hid my relationship with my first boyfriend all the way to my senior year of high school. I was now getting attention from boys, and it felt good. I felt special, beautiful, and important. Although my stepfather was in my life, he didn't have the capacity to love me and guide me the way I needed to be. Much like my mom, he simply laid down strict rules: "Study your school work, don't think about boys." So, when the boy whom I thought was the love of my life broke my heart, I didn't have a dad that I could go to with my broken pieces. I didn't have a dad to console me. My dad would have been my first love, showing and teaching me how a young girl, and eventually woman, should be treated and respected.

In my twenties I didn't know who I was. I think that's

around the time when I realized the connection between losing my father and my constant sense of void. I was empty and attempted to fill this gulf within my soul with men. I wanted to be loved, but no matter what I did, that feeling of emptiness remained, and I was depressed all the time. One day, I decided that things needed to change—I needed to change. I needed to be healed, and I sought therapy.

Therapy opened old wounds. It brought me back to my childhood and allowed me to confront loss. I had the opportunity to now speak openly about my father and as I did so, I realized that much of what I had allowed in my life, much of my actions, were a cry for help.

Grief is a tricky thing. It hides itself in busyness and activities of our lives, and just when we think that we have dealt with loss, accepted it, we find ourselves in a dark place overcome by despair. I did the necessary work in therapy and I am still doing the work. I realized I haven't fully healed from losing my father and may never fully get there. I still wish my dad was here to give me big strong hugs. I wish he was here to give me advice on men and to get his approval on the man I should marry. I wish my dad was here to be a grandfather and role model to my son.

Losing a parent at any age can be indescribable. It may be loss due to death, or loss due to an absentee parent; regardless, the void that you feel can't be replaced by things or people. It was not until I hit my emotional rock bottom that I realized I could never fill it with anything or anyone but God.

You may have experienced loss in your life. Perhaps a parent, or even both parents have passed away. Perhaps, your parents are alive but have not loved you the way you should be loved. Maybe, you live in a single parent household and the absence of your mother or father has left a void. Perhaps you are all too acquainted with loss. If you can relate, below I have shared a few scriptures and an affirmation that have helped me along the way. These scriptures spoke to my heart and I hope they will speak to your heart. Take the time to meditate on them and affirm yourself. In your quiet time, use the area provided to write out scriptures that minister to your soul and help you through your loss. No matter the losses you have faced, God wants to heal you from the inside out. God wants to comfort your broken heart. Today, young lady, I pray that instead of running into the arms of a man, you will run into the arms of a loving Father.

SCRIPTURE ON LOSS

"He will wipe every tear from their eyes. There will be no more death or mourning or crying or pain, for the old order of things has passed away." (Revelation 21:4 NIV)

> *"The Lord is close to the brokenhearted and saves those who are crushed in spirit."* (Psalms 34:18 NIV)

> *"Come to me, all you who are weary and burdened, and I will give you rest."* (Matthew 11:28 NIV)

Affirmation: THE LORD HAS MENDED MY BROKEN HEART AND I AM HEALED.

QUESTIONS TO PONDER:

- Have you experienced loss in your life, if so who?
- Write about the person you lost (writing can be healing).

REFLECTION: Loss of any significant person(s) in your life will be one of the most difficult things you may face. There is no appointed time to stop grieving and you can't get over your loss. As we surrender our hurt and pain, God will comfort our hearts, draw near to him and He will always be there.

LOSS: HOW THE JOURNEY BEGAN

DISCOVERING GOD IN YOU

LOSS: HOW THE JOURNEY BEGAN

CHAPTER 2

DISCOVERING A NEW YOU

I was about to turn forty years of age and I was dealing with all sorts of emotions. This was a major milestone and my feelings were all over the place! On one hand I was grateful for making it to that age. On the other hand, I was overwhelmed with sadness, feeling as if I had not accomplished much. Truthfully, I felt lost. In retrospect, I probably should have opted to start therapy again, but I delayed it. I tried to convince myself to celebrate, "Come on Kim! This is a major milestone. Be happy!" You see, I equated happiness to achievement and was focused on what I didn't accomplish instead of what I did accomplish. At that moment, I felt as if my life had no meaning, and I frankly felt stuck.

I was in the valley of depression and I knew that, heading into my forties, I didn't want to stay there. For so many years, depression was a part of who I was—a part of my being, but I no longer wanted to identify with it. Maybe you have been weighed down by depression for many years. Maybe you are focused on what you don't have instead of focusing on what you do have. Maybe you've lost yourself in your pain. Maybe it's time for you to discover a new you. I had to make up my mind on that birthday that I needed to rediscover and redefine myself.

Discovering a new you starts and ends with God. In seeking my freedom, I drew closer to Him. I believed that I needed to fight for my sanity and my only weapons were God's Word and prayer. I thought that the closer I got to God, that ol' spirit of depression would disappear. But the reality was it crept back into my life from time to time. It was not until I heard a sermon preached by my pastor titled, "Identity Crisis", that I had a real breakthrough. As my pastor preached, all I could think was, "That's me! That's my life! He's talking to and about me!" It was in that moment that I realized I was dealing with an identity crisis. I did not truly know who I was and my purpose. I now had identified the root of my years of struggles, and I knew that there needed to be a shift in my perspective. I made the decision that day to begin to identify myself with the one who created me—God.

Are you dealing with an "identity crisis"? Don't be discouraged. Discovering your identity is a life-long process. Perhaps like me, you have dealt with low self-esteem for many of your young years. Perhaps like me, you have doubted your abilities, talents and gifts. Perhaps men, career and money have defined your identity. I know what that's like. My relationships dictated my happiness and my career identified me as "someone"—I was acceptable to society. But what I realized was that even with numerous accolades, it never felt like enough. I never felt like I was enough. If you can relate to my story, then perhaps you are dealing with an identity crisis.

Young lady, consider this: "You are God's masterpiece" (Ephesians 2:10). Do you believe that? The first step in discovering a new you requires you to believe what God says about you. When God says he "makes all things new" (Revelation 21:5), I had to wrap my mind around it. I had to process it, sit with it and allow myself to believe it. You have to wrap your mind around who God says you are. You have to process it and believe it. You cannot move forward into the life God wants for you believing the lies of the enemy. It's time to believe God.

A new you also requires that you exchange your thoughts for God-thoughts about you, and that's your second step. God sees us as his daughters. You have to see yourself how God sees you. You are precious to Him. You are not defined by the world. You are not who your parents say you are or are not. Yes, my name is Kimberley Juanita Rodney—that's how the world identifies me. However, our Father, the King, says I am royalty, His precious jewel, His masterpiece—the one He created in my mother's womb. Exchanging our thoughts for God's thoughts means that we have to know God's Word. To redefine myself, I had to become familiar with the Word of God. I realized it wasn't enough to go to church on Sundays, and to look like I had faith, but I needed to spend time meditating on God's truths. Discovering a new you requires that you now get rid of your distorted self-view and begin to see yourself through the eyes of the Creator.

The third step in discovering a new you, requires us to see God differently. We have to see God as One who always wants the absolute best for us and loves us unconditionally. When God created us in our mother's womb, He knew every number of hairs on our heads—God knows everything about us. We have to see God as a loving Father, who may not give us everything we desire, but gives us His very best. No matter the mistakes we've made or will make, your Heavenly Father loves you unconditionally. We are perfect in the eyes of God—body and soul, we are marvelously made (Psalm 139:14). God is not waiting to condemn you or beat you down with guilt, but His loving arms are always extended to you. When we see God differently, we can see ourselves differently, because we are made in His image.

Discovering a new you is a process, and although I realized I was dealing with an identity crisis, it was not until heading into my forty-first birthday that I truly began to see the transformation. I've come to the place where I'm realizing more and more that my heart and my soul have to be one with God. Young lady, your heart and your soul have to be one with God. Allow God to redefine you. Allow God to tell you who you are. When you have discovered your true identity through your relationship with God, you will be able to look yourself in the mirror and say, "I am enough!"

God knows your name. He knows what's deep down inside waiting to be revealed. You are a queen. You are beautiful inside and out. When you know who you are, you will not settle for mediocrity. When you know who you are, you will rise to the occasion to lead others to Christ. When you know who you are, you will be able to go further, do more, be more and live for the glory of God. Young lady, you are the apple of God's eye, and when the enemy tries to tell you otherwise, here are some scriptures and an affirmation to remind you of your identity. You are perfectly made in Him!!!

SCRIPTURES ON IDENTITY

"Before I formed you in the womb I knew you [and approved of you as My chosen instrument], and before you were born I consecrated you [to Myself as My own]; I have appointed you as a prophet to the nations." (Jeremiah 1:5 AMP)

> *"I praise you because I am fearfully and wonderfully made; your works are wonderful, I know that full well".*
> (Psalm 139:14 NIV)
>
> *"Therefore, if anyone is in Christ, the new creation has come: The old has gone, the new is here!"* (2 Corinthians 5:17 NIV)

Affirmation: I'M GOD'S DAUGHTER. I AM ROYALTY AND I AM DADDY'S GIRL.

QUESTIONS TO PONDER:

- Who are you?
- Have you struggled with your identity?

REFLECTION: We tend to find ourselves looking for our identity in relationships, career and money, however the more we do that, the more we lose ourselves. Our identity can be only found in God, for he is everlasting.

DISCOVERING A NEW YOU

DISCOVERING A NEW YOU

DISCOVERING GOD IN YOU

CHAPTER 3

DISCOVERING YOUR WORTH

It was another Sunday morning and I was heading out to church. I was ready to hear what the Lord had to say to me, but... I had to make a quick stop. I'd left my nice pair of church shoes at "his" house and needed to grab them. I finally arrived and knocked on the door, but no one answered. I kept knocking, wondering what was happening. Finally, his roommate answered the door, and I ran upstairs to grab my shoes. Trevor, my boyfriend, met me at his door. Typically, I would have full access to his room, but not that morning. That morning, he blocked me from entering. "What are you doing?!", I asked. Still trying to prevent me from entering, I pushed my way in only to be surprised by another woman in his room. I was dumbfounded—shocked, to say the least. Now, while you would have thought that this incident marked the end of our relationship it didn't. I must confess that I stayed with him, year after year, because I didn't know my worth.

As I look back at my young adult years, I can say that I've compromised my worth and value so many times. Not seeing myself how God sees me caused me to make many reckless decisions. I ran from one relationship to another, trying to find that elusive love. For me, a relationship validated me. A man on my arms meant that I was worthy of love—someone wanted me. It didn't matter how bad the relationship was or how unfaithful he was; I was wanted. When you don't know who you are and you don't understand your value, you will settle for anything.

Worth is the value that God placed on you at the point of your conception. Think about this: God made a deliberate decision to give you life on earth. It wasn't unplanned—it was God's divine will that you are here. You were birthed with value, simply because God chose you. But the reality is that, even though you have value, sometimes life experiences will attempt to mask your worth. Abandonment, physical, emotional and sexual abuse—life's traumatic events—may have you feeling worthless.

Discovering your worth begins first with acknowledging behaviors and choices you can admit does not affirm your value. The pains and challenges you have had to experience may have caused you to see yourself as "less than". I can relate, but I also know that unless you identify where you have comprised your value, you are bound to repeat the same patterns. Now that you have discovered a new identity in Christ, it's time to add value to that identity.

I began to understand who I am and my worth when I began getting closer to God. Each time I spent reading the Bible, hearing God's Word in church, connecting with other believers, my perspective about my life, my identity and my worth changed. I realized that God created me to think worthy of myself, and God wants you to do the same. Identify the areas in your life where you have devalued yourself. Have you been staying in a toxic relationship because you think that's the best you can do? Have you allowed opportunities to pass you by because you have doubted your skills? Have you been living below God's best for your life?

If you have been finding your worth in things and people, it's time for you to find your worth through your relationship with God. God is the only One who can truly affirm us. When we draw closer to Him and are totally dependent on Him, He begins to reveal who we truly are. Our worth can be found only in God, and any other source can be detrimental to our lives. I believe that as we develop our relationship with God—spending quality time with Him, renewing our mind with God's Word, and being in constant communication with our Heavenly Father, we will be transformed from the inside out, and our lives will reflect a new sense of worth.

It has taken me many years to recognize my value. I had to be intentional about my relationship with God. I wanted to be transformed and the good news is that once I discovered my worth, I'm much more mindful of the choices and decisions I make. I am happy to say that I have come to a point in my life where I am not allowing anyone or anything, except God, to dictate my worth. Even with all the mistakes I've made, I see myself how God sees me. I now see myself as worthy.

Young lady, you are worthy in spite of your mistakes, your scars and pains. You are worthy in spite of the trauma you have endured. You are worthy in spite of what others have said about you. You are God's handiwork. You are worthy of respect, admiration, happiness, peace and most of all love. God loves you unconditionally—that means no strings attached. When you feel as if you are in a valley, or a dark place allow His love to affirm you. Look in the mirror and remind yourself that you are a diamond, a priceless jewel, a young woman of tremendous worth. See it and believe it. As you continue on your journey to discovering your value within, here are some affirming words and scriptures to remind you that you are worthy.

SCRIPTURES ON WORTH

"And now, my daughter, do not be afraid, I will do for you all that you ask, for all the assembly of my people know that you are a worthy woman." (Ruth 3:11 NRSV)

"You are altogether beautiful, my darling; there is no flaw in you." (Song of Songs 4:7 NIV)

"...Fear not, for I have redeemed you. I have summoned you by name. You are Mine." (Isaiah 43:1 NIV)

> **Affirmation:** I AM WORTHY OF EVERY GOOD THING THAT GOD HAS FOR ME.

QUESTIONS TO PONDER:

- Do you think you are worthy? Why or why not?
- Has there ever been a time where you felt worthless, and if so, when did you get to the point where that changed into seeing yourself as worthy of God's best?

REFLECTION: God created us with such detail, he knows us from every count of hair on our heads. God created us to believe and see ourselves as worthy. Believe that He created us from nothing to something.

DISCOVERING YOUR WORTH

DISCOVERING YOUR WORTH

DISCOVERING GOD IN YOU

CHAPTER 4

DISCOVERING YOUR PURPOSE

April 26, 2018 started as a normal workday. I did my daily routines—got my son out of bed, cooked breakfast, got dressed, jumped in the car and dropped my son off at school. It was a beautiful sunny day and everything was going as planned. I had a few appointments that morning and after my first trip to a client's house, I was off to the second appointment. There I was, driving down a one-way street without a care in the world, and suddenly I heard a loud bang. Before I knew it, my car was spinning out of control, the airbags inflated and smoke was coming from the hood. When the car finally stopped spinning, I was in utter shock. Shaking uncontrollably, I managed to get out of the car only to realize that I had been hit by another car whose driver had not stopped at the stop sign. The day that started so great turned into one the worst days of my life. I could have died, but God saved me. That accident changed my life for the good and bad. I still have to deal with the physical and emotional effects of it—that's the bad part. But, it was that accident that made me realize that I have purpose on earth—that's the good part. When I think back on the things I have gone through, I am grateful that I am still alive. That accident could have killed me. The fact that I am alive on this earth only reminds me that I'm here for a purpose—my work on earth is not yet completed.

At times you may feel as if you are nothing, and that emptiness will try to follow you throughout your life. But I want to remind you that God decided to put you here on this earth for a reason. The fact that you made it through trauma, poor choices and other experiences, means that God has more for you. You have purpose. Purpose is the reason for your existence. Purpose is the reason why you were created the way you are—with your uniqueness; your abilities; your strengths and even your weaknesses. You were created with and for a purpose; however, when you don't recognize it, you will simply go through the ebbs and flows of life with no sense of direction.

When we don't realize that we have purpose, we will feel lost and settle for a life of existing, and not living. Purpose is the fuel that drives us to keep living, keep aiming for better, keep growing, keep reaching for our goals, and living the life that God intends for us to live. You have purpose, but how do you discover it?

Discovering your purpose begins with going before the

Creator and asking Him to reveal the gifts and talents within. It is asking the Creator to show you your place in this earth. Asking God to reveal how you can be all that He created you to be. It is asking God for His desires for your life. Asking God to reveal His plans. Ask and wait on God to reveal His will. Revelation may come in the form of a desire—a strong urge. God may give you an idea to create something or do something. He may use others to confirm your purpose. He will plant a seed within, one that you must water and nurture until it blossoms.

Discovering your purpose is a journey and a process. It is a journey of self-discovery—a journey that I am still on. It is a journey, but it is a beautiful one, because when you discover your purpose, your life will never be the same. When you've received a divine revelation of who you are and who you were created to be, you will begin to walk boldly into your destiny. You will begin to take authority and control over your life. When you know there is purpose on your life, you will begin to slay those God-inspired dreams. When purpose is evident, you don't need validation, affirmation or even encouragement from others, because you know that God has equipped you to do great things. Young lady, do you recognize that you have purpose?

When I look back, I can now see God's divine providence—sustaining, providing and guiding me all throughout my life. He kept me because He had purpose for me, and sharing my story in this book is a part of His plan. It's exciting to know that our lives are purposeful and divinely guided by Christ—knowing He always has our backs. It is purpose that fuels me to live each day as a gift from God. I now realize that I have so much more within, and more to accomplish in this world. I am now a woman who says "yes" to her dreams. I wake up each day with the revelation that because I'm still here, I have work to do. I have purpose as a social worker, helping to change lives. I have purpose as a mother raising a son. There is purpose in being a sister to my siblings, a friend to my friends, a daughter to my parents and a woman of this world. I wake up knowing that I must keep going because I have purpose, and so do you.

Young lady, you have so much more within and so much more to accomplish. God has you in the palm of His hands. You were given purpose within your mother's womb. You are unique in every way, shape and form. God has given you gifts, talents and abilities; recognize them and use them. Don't waste what he has planted inside of you, waiting to be manifested. Rise up, seek God's will and be who He has created you to be—a woman of purpose. As you move forward, affirm yourself with God's Word.

SCRIPTURES ON PURPOSE

> "For I know the plans I have for you declares the Lord, plans to prosper you and not to harm you. Plans to give you hope and a future." (Jeremiah 29:11 NIV)

> "We are God's creation. He created us to belong to Christ Jesus. Now we can do good works. Long ago God prepared these works for us to do." (Ephesian 2:10 NIRV)

> "Many are the plans in a person's heart, but it is the Lord's purpose that prevails." (Proverbs 19:21 NIV)

Affirmation: I AM GIFTED AND TALENTED. GOD HAS CREATED ME WITH PURPOSE.

QUESTIONS TO PONDER:

- Have you struggled with knowing your purpose?
- Why do you think you're here on this earth?

REFLECTION: Every person on this earth has a purpose because God created us with purpose for purpose. When you seek Him with all your heart, your purpose will be revealed.

DISCOVERING YOUR PURPOSE

DISCOVERING YOUR PURPOSE

CHAPTER 5
DISCOVERING FREEDOM

Mental health and wellness is not something we tend to speak openly about. It can be somewhat of a taboo topic, and still so many are struggling. I know what it's like to find it difficult to sleep at night. I know what it's like to have my mind racing, and not being able to rest. I know what it's like to struggle with depression, and to feel like I am not where I should be in life. I know what it's like to struggle to remain happy. As a social worker, I know what it's like to deal with other people's issues, but I also had to recognize that it was necessary for me to deal with my own. As you move forward, young lady, you may face your own mental health struggles, but guess what? It's okay. This final chapter of this book is dedicated to freedom—your freedom, and in order to be free and remain free, we must do the work. This work is both practical and spiritual.

The first practical step toward freedom is to recognize

the mental struggle. Self-awareness is key, so it's important to identify and accept that something is wrong. The next and one of the most important steps is to seek professional help. Therapy has been a conduit of healing for my life. It allowed me to discover repressed pain, unhealthy patterns and so much more. Therapy has been life-changing and through it, I learned how to put me first. You may need to find a therapist to help you work through some of your traumatic experiences. You may not be able to fight all that the enemy throws your way by yourself. People around you may even frown upon the thought of therapy, but regardless of what society says, when you choose to get the help you need, you are choosing to be free. Young Queen, don't shy away from taking the practical steps, but also don't forget to take the spiritual steps.

Therapy, prayer, God's Word and God's presence go hand in hand. For me, true freedom is letting go and letting God lead, guide and heal the areas of my life where I felt most overwhelmed. As life unraveled, and my thought process became scrambled, God revealed to me that I needed to find freedom in Him. When I tried to figure everything out on my own, God reminded me that I'm nothing without Him. God has become my source for all things including the source of my freedom. What areas of your life do you need God to lead, guide and heal? Maybe it is time to give God the control. That's why sustaining your relationship with God is so important, because when you trust the One you are in relationship with, you can trust Him to steer you towards freedom. When God is in control, He may lead you down a path that forces you to confront some things, but at the end of the journey you will discover freedom.

Freedom is also the ability to forgive, to let go of unnecessary drama, and be vulnerable with God and one other. Freedom is the ability to love and support one another. God gave us a heart to chase after Him, but He also gave us a heart to love. Queen, God wants you to be free. Who do you need to forgive? What drama do you need to let go? How can you take a vulnerable step towards freedom? Unforgiveness blocks us from living the life that God wants us to live. Unforgiveness blocks our happiness, peace, and ability to love and be loved. As you take this journey to discover God in you, search your heart and identify any areas that have been blocked by unforgiveness and drama. Queen, God wants you to be free to be who He has created and called you to be. You may have been through some difficult times, but despite what you may have faced in life, you were created to win.

Ladies, freedom is winning in life. Your current life position is not your final destination if you do not give up. To win is to realize that God has more for you. To win is to never give up on your dreams and desires, regardless of your current situation.

Freedom is setting goals and actively working to accomplish those goals. Let God's light shine brightly through you and into this world. Refuse to place limits on yourself, and don't ever place limits on God as He will do exceedingly and abundantly above all you could ever imagine. See yourself free—free from everything that tried to hold you back. See yourself free—free to soar. See yourself free—free to live your best life walking in your purpose. I declare in Jesus name, you are free! There is freedom in knowing who you are and whose you are, and that's winning.

Queen, liberty is what God offers you. No more bondage—nothing is holding you back. I pray that as you continue on this journey, you will walk with your head held high, knowing that your past is behind you and what's ahead is great. I pray that you will live a life that says, "I've been set free and I will be all that God has created me to be." Go forth and as you go, hold on to God's Word and daily affirm yourself. Here are a few scriptures to meditate on along the way. May they remind you that God has you in the palm of his hands and you are indeed free.

Scriptures on Freedom

> *"So if the Son sets you free, you will be free indeed."*
> (John 8:36 NIV)

> *"Christ has set us free to live a free life. So take your stand! Never again let anyone put a harness of slavery on you."*
> (Galatians 5:1 MSG)

> *"Out of my distress I called on the Lord; the Lord answered me and set me free."* (Psalm 118:5 AMP)

Affirmation: I AM FREE FROM MY PAST; FREE TO LIVE AND FREE TO SOAR.

QUESTIONS TO PONDER:

- When have you felt most free in your life?
- Have you ever felt like your life was in shackles?

REFLECTION: At times, we feel our lives are in bondage and the only way out is to ask God to guide you into a life of freedom.

DISCOVERING FREEDOM

DISCOVERING FREEDOM

CHAPTER 6

SOAR!

My sister, discovering who you are through God is a lifelong process and a journey that I am personally still on. Growth takes time and full realization of self may take months and even years. God did not guarantee us an easy, drama-free life, but in fact Jesus said, "...In this world you will have trouble. But take heart! I have overcome the world" (John 16:33). In Christ there is joy, peace, victory and freedom. God has marked you—placed His stamp of approval on you. It does not make a difference where you were born and the circumstances of your life, God says, I created you in my image. You are God's—you belong to the Father. You are the apple of God's eyes (Psalm 17:8 ESV). You are God's beloved. So no matter what society says about you, hold your head high and walk as one loved by the Creator.

Every day I wake up, I thank God that He does not hold my poor choices and my past against me. His love is renewed each day. God is not holding your past against you. When you embark on this journey to discover who God really created you to be, when you do the work to discover your identity, worth, purpose and freedom in God, you will thrive and overcome everything that was designed to keep you living below God's best.

Young lady, I call you blessed. I call you whole. I call you successful. I call you powerful. I call you unique—one of a kind. I call you beautiful. You are a queen, created to reign. You are an eagle, so, go forth and soar, and when the world tells you that you can't, or you shouldn't, declare, "I can and I will because God says so!"

"Trust in and rely confidently on the Lord with all your heart, and do not rely on your own insight or understanding. In all your ways know and acknowledge and recognize Him, and He will make your paths straight and smooth [removing obstacles that block your way]."

(Proverbs 3:5-6 AMP)

SOAR!

SOAR!

CPSIA information can be obtained
at www.ICGtesting.com
Printed in the USA
LVHW020839221022
731316LV00007B/595

9 781736 748367